graffiti culture

Liz Gogerly

Graffiti should only be practised in areas designated to legal graffiti or in a class situation under proper adult supervision.

First published in 2011 by Wayland

Copyright © Wayland 2011

Wayland
Hachette Children's Books
338 Euston Road
London NW1 3BH

Wayland Australia
Level 17/207 Kent Street
Sydney NSW 2000

Concept by Joyce Bentley

Commissioned by Debbie Foy and Rasha Elsaeed

Produced for Wayland by Calcium
Designer: Paul Myerscough
Editor: Sarah Eason

British Library Cataloguing in Publication Data

Graffiti culture. — (Art on the street)(Radar)
1. Graffiti—Juvenile literature.
I. Series
751.7'3-dc22

ISBN: 978 0 7502 6500 3

Printed in China

Wayland is a division of Hachette Children's Books, an Hachette UK company.

www.hachette.co.uk

Acknowledgements: Corbis: Tim Mosenfender 14–15; Flickr: CopperKettle 16, Indieink 24–25, Thomas Locke Hobbs 20r, MrsMullerauh 26c, Los Cardinalos 21r, Bruce Turner 11; Hedz: 2c, 7bc, 7bl, 7c; iStockphoto: Reinhard Kaiser 10; Mosstika.com: Edina Tokodi/Maxim Chelak 27b; Rex: Everett Collection 23, Sipa Press 28; Shutterstock: 3l, 3r, Rob Ahrens 26l, BMCL 8, 2t, Diego Cervo 1, 4–5, 17b, Sam Cornwell 3br, 17t, 18t, Neale Cousland 21l, David Davis cover, Gary 718 12b, Hannamariah 6–7, Juhku 13t, Sergey Kamshylin 12c, L. Kragt Bakker 27t, Jon Le-Bon 17r, Blazej Maksym 7br, Pixel Memoirs 9, Roman Sigaev 26b, Stefanie Mohr 12br, Stefano Tiraboschi 2b, 20l; Wikipedia: 10t.

cover stories

8

STAR STORY
Find out about the life and work of mystery man and artist Banksy

12

BIG DEBATE
Is graffiti art or crime? Join the big debate!

6

5-MINUTE INTERVIEW
Find out why graffiti art is so hot with Radar's expert Stuart Styles

20

WORLD VIEW
Take the graffiti art world tour

CONTENTS

the people

6   **5-MINUTE INTERVIEW** Stuart Styles

8   **STAR STORY** Banksy

10   **THE HISTORY BIT** Writings on the wall

14   **POSTER PAGE** M.I.A.

22   **STAR STORY** David Choe

the art

16   **ZONE IN** Permanent style

18   **SHOW ME** Graffiti tag

24   **DON'T TRY THIS AT HOME!** Shadow graffiti

26   **ZONE IN** Temporary art

the talk

4   **ALL ABOUT** Graffiti

12   **BIG DEBATE** Art or vandalism?

20   **WORLD VIEW** Passport to paint

28   **READ ALL ABOUT IT** Designer graffiti

30   **THE LINGO** Spray-can speak

32   **FAN CLUB** Graffiti, game on!

32   **INDEX**

GRAFFITI

It's eye-catching and it's everywhere. Graffiti can be a simple name tag or a work of art, but the very mention of the word graffiti can kick up a storm. Some people love it, while others think it's a crime. Some think it's about freedom of expression, while others think it defaces the urban environment. Graffiti is controversial, but one thing is for certain – it plays a massive part in modern culture.

In the public eye

The word 'graffiti' means 'scratched' and it can be anything, from words and markings to pictures and symbols. Most artists use spray-cans, paint and chalk to leave their mark on walls and buildings. Graffiti is just about everywhere, from underground stations to tall skyscrapers. In the last few decades, graffiti art has even made its way onto the walls of some of the most famous art galleries. In 2008, London's Tate Modern gallery turned its walls into an open-air canvas for graffiti art. In 2009, the Grand Palais gallery in Paris hosted one of the largest exhibitions of graffiti art ever!

Word on the street

Graffiti has its roots on the street. It gives ordinary people the power to deliver a message or share their thoughts in a visual way. Graffiti often thrives on conflict and resentment against the authorities. For example, in the 1970s, punks used graffiti to get across their anger against the lack of jobs and opportunities for young people at that time.

Painting for peace

Graffiti can also be a powerful tool for delivering messages of peace. Among the political messages on the Berlin Wall and the 'peace line' gates in Northern Ireland there were pleas for peace. To this day, Palestinians spray-paint their peace messages on the Israeli West Bank barrier.

STUART STYLES

Stuart is a leading commercial graffiti artist who runs his own urban art business called Hedz. As well as holding art workshops, Hedz creates stunning commercial artwork. Radar gets together with Stuart to discover more about the graffiti scene.

What do you love about doing graffiti?

Graffiti is the most invigorating and absorbing interest I have ever had. I love it because it's about freedom of expression. It connects with people regardless of location, cultural background or age group.

How do people get into the graffiti scene?

Graffiti is not an art form that you 'accidentally' become involved with. In the past, many artists already knew each other because they were part of a network on the street, which was difficult for new artists to join. These days, internet and media coverage has made it much easier to connect with like-minded people.

What are your top tips for creating awesome artwork?

Researching your artistic ideas is my top tip for achieving amazing results. Most artists get tons of inspiration from the internet. It's also important to share ideas with other artists and young people. Once you have an idea, you've got to keep on practising. When I first started I sometimes had to repeat a painting thousands of times before I was happy!

Have your aerosol antics ever got you into trouble with the police?

No, never. There is no value in creating art in an illegal environment. It can be dangerous and damaging to other people and their property.

Why do you think graffiti is good for our communities?

Graffiti is bright, exciting and colourful – what better way is there to improve a neglected space within our communities? Graffiti art can also communicate some complex messages in a way that brings together people from different race, age and social backgrounds.

Which products feature your graffiti designs?

We create designs for all kinds of products, from clothing and drinks labels to football nets. Our graffiti designs have also been used on TV sets – we designed a graffiti backdrop for one of the Walkers Crisps adverts!

How can kids get involved with urban art?

There's never been a better time for aspiring urban artists to access graffiti culture. I would recommend urban art workshops run in schools, colleges and universities. Young people can gain access to urban culture in a safe and educational environment. It's also a good idea to get online and seek information on Google, YouTube and various youth culture programmes that you can find on TV.

BANKSY

THE STATS

Name: Banksy – real name unknown

Born: Around 1974

Place of birth: Thought to be Bristol, UK

Job: Graffiti artist and political activist

International man of mystery

Some people believe this classic Banksy piece is a political statement – the maid is sweeping the UK's social problems under a curtain.

Check out www.banksy.co.uk to see a collection of his work.

Underground scene

Banksy first got into graffiti in the 1990s on the streets of Bristol, UK. In the early days, he was a freehand artist but he took up stencilling because it was much quicker. Under cover of darkness, the stealthy stencil artist created witty scenes. Favourite subjects included policemen, rats and children. Banksy used these images to get across his anti-establishment feelings. One of the most famous Banksy rats holds a banner supporting anarchism. An image of a policeman searching a young child expresses Banksy's mistrust of the law!

The UK's number one graffiti artist

By the early 2000s, Banksy was the UK's number one graffiti artist. Nobody knew who he was, but more people knew about his art. Spotting 'Banksies' on the streets of Bristol, London and New York was as much a cultural exercise as visiting an art gallery. In 2002, Banksy got a taste of international fame with his first exhibition in LA, USA. He also did the cover artwork for the band Blur's album *Think Tank* and in that year took part in the Semi-Permanent Graffiti and Street Art Exhibition in Sydney, Australia, together with Dmote and Shepard Fairey (two rising stars of the street art world).

The aloof spoof

Banksy has also been behind a series of art pranks. In 2004, he produced wads of spoof £10 notes with 'Banksy of England' on them. In 2005, he planted a fake cave painting at the British Museum in London. The painting looked genuine except it showed a primitive man hunting with a shopping trolley!

Who is Banksy?

Today, Banksy is amongst the most famous graffiti artists in the world. But the big question is, who is he? The truth is that nobody knows for sure. Like many graffiti artists, Banksy keeps his identity a secret. Most graffiti is illegal so it pays to stay underground. And, being a man of mystery seems to just add more to his street appeal!

Career highlights

2008 over three days, Banksy hosted 'The Cans Festival' in Leake Street, London. Graffiti artists from all over the globe brought colour to an abandoned part of the city

2009 Banksy's UK Summer Show opened at Bristol's City Museum and Art Gallery. With over 100 pieces, it was his biggest exhibition to date

2010 produced his first film called *Exit Through the Gift Shop: A Banksy Film*

WRITINGS ON THE WALL

KILROY WAS HERE

It's hip, it's happening and it has the edge. By its very nature, graffiti feels modern and relevant to today's culture. But graffiti is nothing new: throughout history people have scribbled on walls…

This ancient Roman graffiti can still be seen on the Santa Maria church in Rome, Italy.

Timeless graffiti

Ancient civilisations may not have had spray-paints but they shared modern society's need for self expression. Examples of graffiti can be found on all kinds of ancient Greek, Roman, Mayan and Viking sites. The Acropolis in Athens, Greece, is covered in ancient graffiti, including name tags and advertisements. And the ancient Roman site at Pompeii, in Italy, has a fascinating range of graffiti, from witty one-liners to confessions of love!

Paving the way

In sixteenth century Italy, temporary graffiti grew in popularity when street painters, called *madonnari*, created chalk portraits of the Madonna or other religious scenes during holy festivals. Later, in the nineteenth century, street painters in the UK were called 'screevers'. They used coloured chalks to draw on pavements and lived off the donations they got from the passers-by.

World War doodles

The First and Second World Wars triggered plenty of funny graffiti. In the USA during the Second World War, a cartoon man with 'Kilroy was here' appeared on walls and buildings everywhere. In the UK, 'Mr Chad' was popular. He was often accompanied with the lines 'Wot no sugar?', making a light-hearted comment on rationing.

Hip-hop and happening!

It was not until the late 1970s that graffiti as we know it today exploded onto the art scene. In New York, rival street gangs used graffiti to mark their territory and competed to create the most eye-catching art. The same gangs were into hip-hop music. Very soon hip-hop became the soundtrack for graffiti art and graffiti became the signature of hip-hop – it was a marriage made on the streets.

Street to gallery

African American graffiti artist Jean-Michel Basquiat made the leap from the street to the gallery with his art in the 1980s. By the 2000s, graffiti art was no longer out of place in cool art galleries. Today, graffiti artists such as Shepard Fairey, Blu and Banksy are famous all over the world. And artists such as Julian Beever and Daim have taken graffiti to a whole new level with their stunning 3D chalk pavement art.

Many of Shepard Fairey's works deliver a political message, as seen in this collection.

ART OR VANDALISM?

Urban artists believe that graffiti art is all about freedom of expression. They say:

FOR

1. Self expression and freedom to protest is a basic human right – graffiti is a non-violent form of protest or political expression.
2. Urban landscapes can be transformed for the better! Graffiti brightens up run-down areas and decaying buildings.
3. It is a true art form that should be celebrated rather than condemned. These days, graffiti can be seen in art galleries, on designer clothes and accessories and on music labels.
4. We can benefit from graffiti – many community art projects bring people together and give young people a chance to express themselves.
5. Some graffiti artists use chalk, water or other non-permanent methods for their work – where is the harm in that?

AGAINST

Opposers of graffiti think it is a form of vandalism that defaces the urban environment. They say:

1. Graffiti is illegal and the people who carry it out are trespassing and defacing public and private property. Not only are graffiti artists breaking the law, they are also making places look ugly.

2. Some artists use bad language or express views that can be offensive to the public. Sometimes the images can be rude or offensive, too.

3. It costs millions to remove graffiti from urban areas. This money could be spent more effectively on making cities better places to live.

4. Graffiti is bad for business. Shops and other businesses that are defaced by graffiti may lose customers because they think the shop looks neglected or downmarket.

5. Graffiti sends out a message that an area is crime-ridden and therefore frightens people away.

RIGHT OR WRONG?

Some people view graffiti as art, others think it is a crime against society. Graffiti remains against the law in most places. Some authorities compromise by creating 'graffiti zones' (where artists are allowed to spray). Others give prison sentences for known offenders. Right or wrong, graffiti art looks set to remain a hotly-debated topic!

M.I.A.

Starting out

Maya was born in London but when she was six months old, her Tamil parents moved back to Sri Lanka. The family then stayed in the war-torn country for the next nine years. As a political activist, Maya's father was rarely around. In 1986, Maya's mother returned to south London with her two daughters as refugees.

THE STATS

Name: Mathangi 'Maya' Arulpragasam
Born: 18 July 1975
Place of birth: London, UK
Nationality: British
Job: Rapper, singer, songwriter, record producer, artist

Spray-paint inspiration

In 2001, Maya wowed the crowds at her first public art exhibition held at a shop on Portobello Road, London. All the influences of her early life were laid bare in a series of vibrant spray-paint and stencil canvases. The war scenes from her childhood were reflected in the graffiti-style tigers, palm trees and freedom fighters. Soon after this, Maya was nominated for the Alternative Turner Prize. Although she looked set to have a successful art career, she decided instead to focus on music.

Film, fashion and fascinating rap

As a teenager, Maya mixed with other Bengali children in the Brick Lane area of East London. In her early twenties, she took a degree in fine art, film and video at London's Central Saint Martins College. She shared a flat with Justine Frischmann, frontwoman of the band Elastica. Justine commissioned Maya to create the cover of Elastica's album *The Menace* (2000).

Prize-winning artist

These days, Maya is an award-winning rapper and recording artist. In 2004, she broke through with singles *Galang* and *Sunshowers*. Since then she has been nominated for Brit, Grammy and Mercury Prize awards. Meanwhile, her background in graffiti gives her live shows, fashion and music artwork an exciting edge. Daring and outspoken, Maya is one of the most exciting artists of recent times and a political voice to be reckoned with.

PERMANENT STYLE

Whether it is covering a wall 'back-to-back' or 'dressing up' a door, some graffiti artists want their work to last. Look out for these permanent styles.

Edgy etching

This style of graffiti can leave permanent scars! Also known as 'scratchiti', the artist uses a sharp object, such as a stone, to scratch or etch into a material.

Tagging

The tag is the simplest and most common type of graffiti. It is the graffiti artist's 'signature' or nickname as a design. Each artist develops their own style and usually sticks to one palette of colour.

etching

Stencilling by stealth

Graffiti artists often work against the clock and under cover of darkness. Stencil graffiti is one way to pull off some nifty pieces in double-quick time – the same piece can be repeated over and over with minimal effort!

Spray-paint at the ready

Graffiti artists sometimes call their spray-can paints 'cannons' – which implies serious business! Spray-paint art is long-lasting and eye-catching. Graffiti opponents view spray-paint as public enemy number one because it is so difficult to remove.

Type 'cans festival london' into www.youtube.com to see a selection of amazing stencil art.

tagging

stencilling

spray-paint

GRAFFITI TAG

Your tag should stand out in a crowd, so it is important to get it just right. You want something cool and unforgettable – a tag that's guaranteed to turn heads!

You will need:

- paper • pencils • marker pens
- imagination and creativity

1 Think about the tag you want to create – what do you want it to say about you?

2 Write your tag in large letters on a piece of paper. Play around with the size and shape of the letters.

3 Experiment with the thickness of the lines and add shading to give the letters a 3D effect.

4

Get out your marker pens and fill in the letters. Be as creative as you can with the colours.

5

Add detail to your tag – but try not to get too carried away because sometimes the simplest tags are the best!

Got it?

Check out the finished article – would you be proud to leave this mark on your personal belongings? Keep practising and collect your tags in your own graffiti design scrapbook.

PASSPORT TO PAINT

The world is the graffiti artist's canvas. Any urban space is an inviting place for artists to make their mark. From the war-torn streets of Tehran in Iran to the metropolis of Tokyo in Japan, urban artists are hard at work…

Graffiti capital New York (left) is famous for its colourful urban art, while São Paulo stairways (above) are covered with murals.

The graffiti capitals

Tags and 'throw-ups' are part of the urban scene in many cities of the world, but some are plastered with graffiti. To tour the streets of New York is to get a taste of how graffiti has evolved since the 1970s. There are murals with a political message, tags from the 'kings' of the hip-hop scene and buildings covered with 'bombings'. Other graffiti capitals include Melbourne, Berlin, Paris, London, Bristol and São Paulo.

The streets of São Paulo

Anyone visiting São Paulo in Brazil should take one of the graffiti tours. The buzzing South American city is a hotbed of cool graffiti. At every turn there is a colourful mural, a blaze of letters or an innovative piece. Some people liken the scene in São Paulo to New York in the 1970s. The city certainly shares some of New York's problems such as poverty, unemployment and urban decay, all of which are expressed in its graffiti art.

Type 'Berlin Wall graffiti' into www.youtube.com to see examples of amazing graffiti art.

Much of the stencil graffiti in Melbourne (below) is designed to make a political or social statement. A Parisian 'graffiti gangster' wears hip-hop jewellery emblazoned with the city's name (below right).

Aussie art

Some people call Melbourne, Australia, the 'stencil capital of the world' because its pavements and buildings feature some of the best stencil graffiti you will find. One of the stars of the local scene is a female graffiti artist called Vexta. She stands out in a predominantly male world. As well as stencil art, she's famous for her stickers and paste-ups.

Art attack in Paris

France has legal graffiti sites all over the country with some exciting spaces within its parks in Paris. However, graffiti is a product of the streets and probably always will be. In fact, an anonymous artist has been at large in Paris since 2010. In response to the French government's ban of the Muslim veil in public, this artist adds veils to the fashion advertisements on giant billboards across the city!

21

DAVID CHOE

King of the 'dirty' style

Art therapy

David Choe grew up in the tough neighbourhood of Koreatown in LA, USA. His parents were Korean immigrants who had their own property business. David was a typical boy, interested in superheroes and *Star Wars* movies. Then, at the age of 14, he discovered graffiti. Over time, art became a form of therapy for David, as graffiti helped him to deal with the difficulties of growing up in a troubled society where crime and race wars were common.

On the road

When he finished high school, David travelled in the USA, Europe and Africa. After two years on the road he enrolled at the California College of Arts. It was here that he developed a method of

painting with almost any medium, from spray-paint and crayons to oil – all layered on top of each other. David called this style of graffiti his 'dirty' style, and it has become his signature.

Doing time

In 2003, David served a three-month jail sentence for a minor offence. During this time, he experimented with his art and began to use different and unusual materials such as soy sauce and even blood! This spell in prison made David think differently about his life, and when he returned to LA he found peace in his work. David then began to exhibit his art and accepted commissions. In 2004, he created the cover for the Jay-Z and Linkin Park CD *Collision Course*, then in 2005 and 2007 David created artwork for the Facebook offices.

Barack and beyond

In 2008, David hit the big time when he created his *Hope* piece for the then future president of the USA, Barack Obama. The same year, David became a star of his own TV travel show *Thumbs Up*, which trails the graffiti artist on his adventures around the world. David and his dirty art made such fascinating viewing that the programme has run for three series. Despite being a hugely successful commercial artist and muralist, David is still drawn to his first love – street graffiti.

Career highlights

1999 self published the cult classic graphic novel *Slow Jams*

2007 commissioned to create the sets for the comedy drama *Juno*

2011 Mark Zuckerberg asked David to create a new painting for the Facebook offices in California, USA

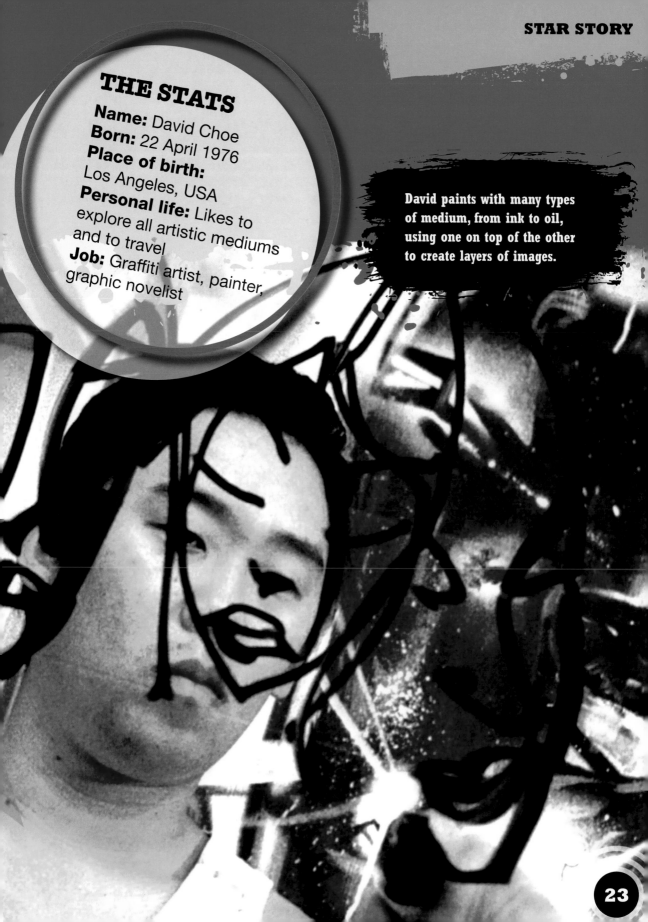

THE STATS

Name: David Choe
Born: 22 April 1976
Place of birth:
Los Angeles, USA
Personal life: Likes to explore all artistic mediums and to travel
Job: Graffiti artist, painter, graphic novelist

David paints with many types of medium, from ink to oil, using one on top of the other to create layers of images.

SHADOW GRAFFITI

Most public graffiti is illegal. However, some local authorities or property owners don't mind chalk graffiti. Chalk washes away easily, so many people don't see it as a problem. Chalk can be used to create stunning shadow graffiti. This art form is not as common as paint graffiti but the idea is catching on…

Essential technique

- Sunshine or street lights is a must to create strong shadows
- Quick on the draw: shadows move quickly and so should the artist!

HOW IT'S DONE

1. The artist finds a suitable subject. Beginners often go for something that has a strong outline and is easy to copy, such as a street sign or a tree.
2. Using light strokes, the artist chalks around the shadow in white.
3. Once happy with the outline of the shadow, the artist colours it in using black chalk.

Why do it?

Shadow graffiti creates a stunning image that attracts attention from passers-by. People question whether the shadow is real or imaginary. The ultimate goal of any art piece is to make people stop and stare, and shadow graffiti does just that!

TEMPORARY ART

chalk

reverse graffiti

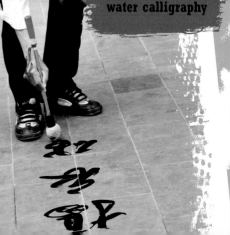

water calligraphy

Type 'Greenpop reverse graffiti forest.mp4' into www.youtube.com to see clean graffiti artists at work.

As governments around the world have cracked down on graffiti, some artists have turned to non-permanent forms of graffiti. They have ditched the spray-paint and marker pens to experiment with chalk, water, stickers, grass and even moss!

Chalk talk

Chalk is bio-degradable and washes away in the rain. For this reason, local authorities rarely prosecute anyone caught using chalk, so young artists often use it for drawing tags. Chalk can also be blended to create different shades. This makes for magnificent examples of 3D art.

'Clean' graffiti

Reverse graffiti is also known as clean-tagging, clean graffiti, dust-tagging or grime writing. All that is required is a dirty surface – such as a window, vehicle or wall. The artist writes a message or design using a fingertip in the dirt. Artists can also clean an area using pressure washing.

Writing in water

All that a water calligraphy artist needs is a large brush, a bucket of water and a pavement on which to write. A message is daubed onto the pavement using the brush and water, and within minutes the words fade away. It is simple but magical to watch.

Sticker bombing

The graffiti artist writes or prints a tag, message or design onto a sticker. The stickers can then be stuck anywhere, from walls and street lamps to billboards and schoolbags.

Going green

Natural products, such as moss and grass, can be used to create the ultimate green graffiti. Artists simply stick the moss or grass to a wall using bio-degradable products. They use this technique to create different words and images.

sticker bombing

moss art

US actress AnnaLynne McCord adds street to her style with a fluorescent graffiti handbag.

DESIGNER GRAFFITI

From graffiti trainers to designer labels incorporating urban art into their clothes, a bond between graffiti and fashion has developed. But when did this relationship begin? And where will it end?

Spray-paint success

In the 1980s, graffiti grabbed the limelight and the craze for daubing the urban landscape took off. It was not long before bold lettering and vibrant graffiti pieces were brightening up clothes. First came big T-shirts decorated with graffiti. One graffiti fashion success story is designer Marc Ecko. He set up his fashion company in 1993 with just six T-shirts and a can of spray-paint. Today, he is head of the billion-dollar fashion and lifestyle company Marc Ecko Enterprises.

Artists at the ready

Graffiti artists have also got in on the act. New York artist Erni Vales became involved in the luxury end of fashion when he designed a range of graffiti handbags. Another big name in the New York graffiti scene who has turned her tag to gold is Claw Money. Her infamous 'claw' logo is actually the 'throw-up' she used to paint on walls. These days it decorates T-shirts, shoes, bags and baby clothes.

Ultimate make-over

One of the most exciting crossovers between graffiti and fashion has to be the Louis Vuitton Graffiti collection. Fashion designer Marc Jacobs was looking for a way to revamp Vuitton's traditional handbags and luggage. Jacobs remembers coming up with the idea of using graffiti artist Stephen Sprouse: 'How do I do something different? … the idea of Stephen Sprouse's graffiti on canvas – defacing something respected and venerable – was very bold. But it also felt right.'

Urban art fever

In 2011, fashion label Moschino treated us to the graffiti jacket for men and the graffiti summer dress for women. But the use of urban art is not restricted to designer labels. In 2011, UK high street chain Marks and Spencer launched the Hello Kitty Graffiti top for girls. Which just goes to show that urban art is alive on the catwalk and kicking on the high street – a sure sign that graffiti fever is here to stay...

SPRAY-CAN SPEAK

Add graffiti cool to your street speak – follow the Radar guide!

aerosol
a can with a spray device that releases liquid, such as paint, from inside the can

back-to-back
a term used by urban artists to describe graffiti that covers a wall from one side to the other

bombing
to thoroughly cover an area in graffiti

calligraphy
the art of producing beautiful or stylised handwriting and lettering

canvases
pieces of canvas fabric that have been stretched and prepared for artists to work on

dressing up
to cover an area, such as a door or wall, that has not been painted before

font
a specific style of lettering

freehand artist
an artist who paints without the guide of a device such as a stencil

king
an artist that is admired for his or her work and owns the most tags in a certain area

mark
to tag or write graffiti

paste-up
an extremely large sticker made by a graffiti artist and pasted onto a wall or other urban surface

piece
a term used by graffiti artists for a painting, which is actually short for masterpiece

run
the length of time a piece of graffiti remains on view to the public before it is covered up by other graffiti or removed

stencil
a sheet of material, such as paper or card, that has a design cut out of it

sticker
a type of non-permanent graffiti. The artist adds anything (from their tag to more elaborate pieces) onto adhesive stickers

tag
a graffiti artist's basic style of signature, a little like their own 'logo'

3D art
three-dimensional letters and images

throw-up
a graffiti term for an image that mostly consists of an outline and one fill-in colour

top-to-bottom
a piece that extends from the top-to-bottom of a train carriage, wall or building

GLOSSARY

Acropolis
an ancient city built high on a hill in the Greek capital of Athens

anarchism
a state in which there are no rules or laws

anti-establishment
against the government and other powers that control society

authorities
the people who have the power to make decisions

Berlin Wall
the wall that divided West Germany from East Germany from 1961 to 1989

bio-degradable
a term used to describe materials that rot away naturally

commercial graffiti artist
an artist who is paid to create graffiti art

commissioned
to be asked to create a piece of art on behalf of another person or organisation

controversial
something that is likely to cause disagreement

hip-hop
a style of music and dance that originated in the 1970s in the USA

Israeli West Bank barrier
the separation barrier that was erected between Israel and Palestine from 2002 onwards

Madonna
The Virgin Mary, who according to Christian belief is Jesus' mother

Mayan
a race of people who lived in South America from 2000 BCE to 900 CE

murals
pictures painted on walls

palette
a range of colours

'peace line' gates, Northern Ireland
the series of separation barriers constructed in Northern Ireland to divide Catholic and Protestant areas

political activist
someone who is involved in politics and seeks to bring about change

Pompeii
the ancient Roman town near Naples in Italy that was destroyed in 79 CE after Mount Vesuvius erupted

race wars
fights between groups of people from different ethnic backgrounds

refugee
a person who seeks shelter in another country because he or she fears persecution based on race, religion or political beliefs

spoof
something that copies an original in a funny way

symbol
a picture that represents something else by association, for example, a dove is a symbol of peace

Tamil
a person who originates from Southern India or North East Sri Lanka

underground
hidden or secret; not well known to many people

urban
relating to a city

vandalism
the malicious and intentional destruction of public or private property

GRAFFITI, GAME'ON!

People to talk to

If the spray-can is calling you, here are just a few of the organisations that can help get your graffiti show on the road without running into trouble…

Hedz

One of the most exciting creative art organisations in the UK, Hedz specialises in commissioned urban art and graffiti and offers workshops, tuition and team-building exercises. Find it at:
www.hedz.ltd.uk

Graffiti Workshop

This organisation runs graffiti workshops in schools, youth clubs and in homes. Find it at:
www.graffitiworkshop.co.uk

Arty reads

Some great graffiti artists have done the hard work, now you colour it in! *Graffiti Colouring Book*, Dokument, 2009

Stencil 101: Make your mark with 25 reusable stencils and step by step instructions, Ed Roth, Chronicle Books, 2008

The mystery artist and his work *Banksy: Wall and Piece*, Century, 2006.

Arty apps

Practise your graffiti anytime, any place with this selection of graffiti apps:

Chalk Draw! • DustTag • Friend Doodle • Graffiti Analysis • Graffiti Draw • Graffiti Spray-Can

INDEX

ancient graffiti 10

Banksy 8–9, 11

chalk graffiti 4, 10–11, 12, 24–25, 26–27

'clean' graffiti 26–27

David Choe 22–23

designer graffiti 12, 28–29

etching 16

'green' graffiti 27

illegal graffiti 4, 9,13, 24

M.I.A. 14–15

murals 20, 22

political messages 5, 8, 12, 15, 20

shadow graffiti 24–25

spray-cans/paint 4–5, 10, 13, 15, 16–17, 27, 29

stencils 9, 15, 16–17, 21

stickers 21, 27

tags 4, 10, 16–17, 18–19, 20, 27, 29

water graffiti 12, 26–27

your mission:
To seek out more cool Radar reads...

BOARD SPORTS
theboarders
thetricks
thegear
978 0 7502 6459 4

FREE RUNNING
therunners
themoves
thefreedom
978 0 7502 6458 7

FREESTYLE BMX
thebikers
thestunts
thebuzz
978 0 7502 6457 0

STREET FOOTBALL
theplayers
theskills
thegames
978 0 7502 6460 0

bhangra & bollywood
thebeat
thestars
theglamour
978 0 7502 6442 6

capoeira
theplayers
themoves
thestory
978 0 7502 6455 6

ice dancing
theskaters
thestars
theglitz
978 0 7502 6456 3

latin dance
thedancers
thesteps
theheat
978 0 7502 6454 9

street dance
thepeople
themusic
themoves
978 0 7502 6441 9

More Radar titles coming soon!

The Armed Services
The Special Forces
Undercover Operations
Police Forensics
Being a Pro Footballer
Being a DJ
Being a Stuntman

Being a Snowboarder
Being a Model
Being a Formula 1 Racing Driver
Celebrity Make-up Artist
Celebrity Fashion Stylist
Celebrity Photographer

Are you on the Radar?